*Then one of the elders said to me,
'Don't cry, look! The Lion from Judah's Tribe, the great
descendant of David, has won the victory and he can
break the seven seals and open the scroll'*

(Revelation 5:5)

THE SCROLL

by

DESHINA DAVIDSON

(The 'God- anoined' Christ and Messiah)

THE SCROLL

(CHARTER FOR *"THE NEW EARTH KINGDOM"* OF THE HOLY SPIRIT)

As Imparted Unto:

DESHINA DAVIDSON

"When a great truth once gets abroad in the world, no power on earth can imprison it, or prescribe its limits, or suppress it. It is bound to go on till it becomes the thought of the world."

- Frederick Douglass (1817 – 1898)

(Writer and orator).

INTRODUCTION

"He that overcometh shall inherit all things; and I will be his God, and he shall be my son"

- (Rev 21:7)

Sometime about 1987, the LORD GOD began to favor me with visits in my sleep and in visions. He had very complimentary remarks for me and concluded that I was above board, "Good." For this one quality, He asked one night that I name my prize.

I had not experienced such behest before, but I knew He really meant well. It dawned on me to prove Him if He really was loving and could bless! So, I asked that He blessed me with, "Half the world!"

God being God, He rather replied: "I'll give you everything!"

Flabbergasted, He requited of me the particular gift I wanted. Wondering what to request, a familiar voice sounding like my late grandmother's said, "Say money." And I not thinking said that.

Thinking God would be angry now, I was again flabbergasted to the contrary when He asked, "How much money?"

Not believing my luck, I thought deep in my little mind's eye for what would beat even the most magnanimous Being – if indeed this was really Almighty God! So I asked for: "Two hundred billion Dollars!"

And God being God again, He rather replied, "I'll make it three hundred."

At this juncture, I sat up and wiped my eyes. Could I really be talking with the Almighty God of Heaven? Or was I just dreaming? I then began to ponder over what I could do with three hundred billion! How could it come about? Where was it stacked in the world? It blew my mind!

God must be pulling my legs, I concluded. Here was I – a necessitous wretch – suddenly offered KING! Who ever heard of such? How was it to be? I started thinking. Then I backed out as I could not make it out.

As though God was all the while reading my mind, He then asked, "How would you like to be so blessed?"

As then a miserable university undergraduate studying Finance, I quickly replied, "In business."

"But you have no business," He retorted. And I withdrew again defeated.

That self-same spirit of my grandmother's again interjected that I say, "In luck." And encouraged again, I did that.

Overwhelmed again, God said He heard. He assured me He would grant, "Everything!" as said. What things He made me realize included a mixed bag of blessings. Some of which is: wisdom, health, wealth, glory, power, honor, knowledge, kingship, dynasty, etc…which summarily would result into my adoption unto Son-ship with Him as "Jesus Christ!" The logic being that everything God had belonged to Jesus Christ His Son. And if I had to inherit all these as "victor", I had to infuse into this Son Jesus. Thereby I became blessed and anointed 'Jesus Christ' incarnate, or the 'Messiah.'

God also then concluded I would have to, "Suffer first."

Thereafter that day and episode things grew worse and worse still. Everything promised turned a delusion and a mirage. I had poor health, learning difficulties, virtual disappointments, ill-luck, hardships, sight and speech impairments, hallucinations, thought blockages, psychomotor disturbances, and closed-doors. Everything just went wacky and zany at first with a deluge of acid-like unpleasantness in my head for several years until mid-May, 2017. And every favor promised of God (or by man) was jinxed and prone to fail like as Job in the Bible.

I sooner also realized I had become schizoid and paranoid with spirits in riotous communion with me to the extent that I was confused. My doctors said I suffered Schizophrenia, but God rather claimed to have poured His "spirits" upon me to conform unto the Son. And I was in God's reckoning under tutelage and mentorship! Given the odds I fought very frantically in an attempt to breakthrough from all the spirits that seemed to jinx me, to no avail.

Later in some of our constant communions, God sealed a "Bond" in **"HOLY TRINITY"** with me, Himself and the Holy Spirit! And this "Covenant" was never to be broken or reversed eternally by the Three. It made me officially the "Christ", and the clasp of the hands was the insignia of it.

As days entered into months and months into years, I persevered in spiritual and medical treatment. At some much later time in counseling, I discovered most so-called "normal" people I told my plight of being Jesus Christ and of controlling all that belonged to God, thought it odd and outrageous and wrote me off for a joker. They claimed Christ will not come again as a pauper and a wacko from the earth below, but in the clouds above gloriously from heaven. They rather aptly dubbed me the "anti-Christ", and would have nothing to do with me.

I often times went back to God dejected and confused, and someday the Spirit took me to the book of Jeremiah 27:5, which goes: *"By my great power and strength, I created the world, mankind, and all the animals that live on the earth; and I give it to anyone I choose."* With referring to this and other Scriptures interspersed all over the Bible as I studied – as: Revelation 12:5, Rev. 21:7, John 10:24 - 38, Malachi 3:1, Rev. 19:7, Isaiah 53:10-12, Hebrews 12:2, etc., etc. - and my articles (which are compiled in this book), I was ever pacified or reassured for that moment that I was not the "anti-Christ" as labeled, but indeed the Christ!

This work attests to and proves this claim in that its seals document the contents of *The Little Scroll* that was handed down to John by the Holy Spirit in Revelation, chapter 10 (but commanded kept secret until as revealed now). It is same as the Lamb of God alone could take from 'Him who sits upon the Throne' and open in Revelation, chapter 5. Its seven-seal contents are indeed the blue-print for *the New Earth kingdom* promised by God variously in the Holy Bible. These seals are new socio-political and economic discourses in solution to seven problem-solving scenarios. They were formulated by me with the help of God while being ill. Some submissions have earlier been published at the instance of the Spirit in certain tabloids and broadsheets, however to little impact. They are now compiled together under this heading, after God has fully restored my health and with the charges to: *"order and establish the Kingdom of God on earth"*; and to *"further the advancement of knowledge."*

My testimony would be incomplete if I do not instruct that whatever errors, commissions, or omissions are inherent in these essays are mine. I personally have had to study hard and with great difficulty to expound whatever I skimmed off books and through discourses under the Holy Spirit's influence. Note also that I'm not certificated in all these subjects, nor have ever studied them all formally neither in my carrier, nor at any point in my life. God however has helped my understanding and insights, being my Guide. I do not therefore affect perfect knowledge on any of these subjects, and is subject to err. God nonetheless considers me sufficiently knowledgeable after haven gone through literature and the grind mill of His tutelage to come out "Doctor" from His school.

The work may engender some controversies– God after all Himself enjoins us to, *'come and let us reason together …'* (Isaiah 1:18). If anyone has a comment or other to make, let them contact the author:

deshina.davidson@yahoo.com

 twitter: @christdeshina

facebook: deshinadavidson

Telephone: +2347013663494, +2348109279841.

Grace be with you and keep the faith.

Deshina Davidson (April, 2017).

ACKNOWLEDGEMENTS AND DEDICATION

"I have always been a learner and am grateful to everyone who has been my teacher."

- (Sirach 51:17).

Although most of the ideas generated in this book are original, they are not all absolutely ingenious or novel. God mostly has imparted them unto me and I have fine-tuned and expounded them through study and reason. In the light of this therefore, I would firstly and most importantly thank and honor God who blesses me with all wisdom, knowledge and understanding for these and many more. I also thank and honor the Holy Spirit who teaches and reminds me all that I've ever been taught. Then I thank the authors of the Good News Bible, which mostly is quoted in this work, and commend their great zeal and effort or conscientiousness to duty in compiling it all. Many thanks also to other version interpreters for their great diligence and commitment to providing diverse meanings and interpretations. Also in this regard, all dedicated ministers and workers in the vineyard of God deserve and reserve my respect in no small measure for nurturing me up in the grace and knowledge of our Lord and Savior Jesus Christ and in the Bible.

The Scroll is a book in dedication to the glory of the Trinity of God the Father, Holy Spirit, and Son. It is in furtherance of the advancement of knowledge; and the establishment and ordering of the Kingdom of God on Earth from now hence - which all, the Father promises to work out with His determination, power and zeal. (Isaiah 9:7).

On a last note, I would like to leave us in contemplation of the subtle benedictions of Jesus son of Sirach in the book of Sirach (Ecclesiasticus), chapter 50, verses 28-29: *"May God bless everyone who gives attention to this work. Whoever takes them to heart will become wise.*

Whoever lives by them will be strong enough for any occasion, because he will be walking in the light of God."

Again, to the TRINITY of God, is all the glory!

DESHINA DAVIDSON

(May, 2017)

TABLE OF CONTENTS

Title page   ii

Introduction   iii

Acknowledgements and Dedication   viii

PROLOGUE   11

SEALONE   12

Towards God's Millennial Reign of Peace

SEALTWO   17

The Political Question and God's Answer

SEALTHREE   27

The Crime and Insecurity Problem and God's Solution

SEAL FOUR   32

God's New Common Wealth

SEAL FIVE   39

Gearing and Sustaining Development God's Way

SEAL SIX   43

Legal Reforms by God

SEAL SEVEN   51

Church Reforms by God

EPILOGUE   55

PROLOGUE

The LORD says, "Here is my servant, whom I strengthen – the one I have chosen, with whom I am pleased. I have filled him with my spirit, and he will bring justice to every nation.

…And now the LORD God says to his servant,

I, the LORD, have called you and given you power to see that justice is done on earth. Through you I will make a covenant with all peoples; through you I will bring light to the nations.

You will open the eyes of the blind and set free those who sit in dark prisons.

I alone am the LORD your God. No other god may share my glory; I will not let idols share my praise.

The things I predicted have now come true. Now I will tell you of new things even before they begin to happen".

- (Isaiah 42:1, 5(d) – 9).

SEAL ONE

TOWARDS GOD'S MILLENNIAL REIGN OF PEACE

"He will settle disputes among great nations. They will hammer their swords into ploughs and their spears into pruning knives. Nations will never go to war again, never prepare for battle again"

- (Isaiah 2:4)

Peace can be defined as a state of tranquility or freedom from war and strife. This can be as a consequent of a pact, truce, or agreement signaling an end to wars and hostilities and the making of peaceful relationships. In order to proffer our solutions to the peace and war problems in the world, we generally need first to understand the three major arguments put forward by debaters in international relations to help build peace and bring about peaceful co-existence amongst nations.

One school in peace and conflict studies has it that an absolute power or nation can preserve the peace simply by policing (or lording it) over weaker nations - as it is today with the United States and the rest nations.

Another argument had it – during the just gone 'cold war' era - that preferably two or more polar powers should be in rivalry to maintain peace.

A third rife debate is for a 'balance' or 'leveling' of powers. At best this is ideal; but the modalities for its attainment are as varied as there are those in support.

At this juncture we rest the debates to proffer our own in support of this last (third) argument and chart a sustainable way out for it:

In our own arguments, we want to suggest two things together: First of which is a *"coming to truce."* Then next secondly, an equalization, balance, or *"parity of powers"*, as we call it. This twain we envisage should help check the tide of wars in the world and hopefully help keep peace on the planet!

Adjunct to this, to our mind, conflicts and wars are predicated on three things: Lack of understanding, lack of tolerance, and keeping of confidences. And thus therefore, our arguments to help build universal peace and to keep peace permanently in the earth is founded upon the threesome of greater and more cohesive mutual understanding, tolerance, and openness.

By "coming to truce" we mean this to be: the galvanized efforts by all nations and factions to end wars or come to ceasefire by extending the "olive branch" to their enemies. Ardently, what we ask is that all nations keep peace by declaring peace treaties one with another. This should be started urgently and universally. What is uttermost are for all nations to kick-start this clamor by means' of positive stoppage of wars among them and bringing to an end all hostilities. Nations, needless to say, must be committed and rededicated to this orchestrated reconciliation or conciliations by compromises, armistices, dialogue and diplomacy - this is how we mean by 'coming to truce!'

Once all nations have embraced peace or come to truce they then may balance [equal up] their powers through the concerted and cooperative efforts of cross-mutually and multilaterally inter-exchanging (or integrating) their soldiers. Their armies thereby no longer then shall be in their obtrusive control to manipulate to cause infractions or insurgences internally or externally any longer. And thereby shall this give rise to a 'parity' or balance of powers, with no nation having superior force or power over another, or nation having inferior force or power to another; and all nations thus seeming to have unitary or level power and parallel supremacy. This, thus further helping to achieve such ideals of equality of all nations in the interstate system of the world as endorsed in the UN Charters.

Evidently as nations of the world come to truce and enter the agreements to neutralize their powers by closing ranks and interchanging soldiers under the parity of powers agenda, thus shall there be peace entrenched in the international body polity. These military exchanges could be carried on just as diplomatic emissaries are interchanged amongst nations. In the light of this, the exchanges should strictly only concern personnel -and not armories or hardware! And it may be delimited to commissioned (or senior) officers only to save costs and the logistics. The officers in themselves may be deployed to serve in any capacities appropriate in their postings. This should help check and cancel out espionage and confidentiality which lead to distrust and wars. It should also help foster international tolerance and cross-mutual understanding needed to check wars and infractions or insurgencies.

Invariably as this is put in place transparency, synergy, unity, and trust would thus have been co-opted. War would have become un-enabled - raising hopes of international peace and security, as this becomes the in-thing. Nations shall then have no need to stockpile or build armories (overtly or covertly) for wars again. Eternal peace shall have reign in the earth (as by our definitions) and rivalry or power struggle fizzled out permanently. Peoples and nations will commingle joyfully together, building bridges of friendship and oneness - globalizing the earth yet still!

Recourse to disenfranchisement from the peace pacts and cooperation once enlisted shall be encumbered and seen as an anti-social act in the eye of the international community. (Needless to mention also, an attack on any one of these nations in this accord would risk a reprisal from all uniformly in its defense).

Since this is an international initiative, administration is best vested on an international body as the UN for organizational purposes only. The UN Secretariat, Secretary-General, or Security Council has no control over it. Control and sponsorship come from the home governments in the domiciled nations and may be channeled through their defense attaches in their diplomatic missions in the host countries. Pertinently also, this is not expected to be as the North Atlantic Treaty Organization (NATO), or the Economic Community of West Africa Monitoring Group (ECOMOG), etc., which are regional or exclusive, and ad-hoc. It is instead to be more inclusive, global and permanent.

One foreseeable clog in the wheel of its workability would probably be that of communication. This could be assuaged probably by standardizing and universalizing military commands. This way the soldiers would be better able to work together, and cooperatively.

The twains ideals of "coming to truce" and "parity of powers" shall therefore both inadvertently have solved the peace and war problems in the world. And as planet earth becomes trouble-less and tranquil, God's love and dominion no doubt shall have enveloped her. All we then are saying is: ***let's keep peace on earth and let it begin right away with each and every one of us!***

We hope this should challenge all men of goodwill, purpose, and right thinking the world over to put into action quickly to free us all from the horrors of future and on-going wars. And maybe someday we shall *"hammer our swords into ploughs and spears into pruning knives"* to usher in God's millennium of peace as foreseen by some Prophets in the Bible.

The model below helps our understanding of the peace initiatives in a microcosm 3-nation world. Imagine the nations to be Austria or Australia, Burundi or Bulgaria, Chile or Cuba, representing countries: A, B, and C, as given.

EXAMPLE ORGANOGRAM FOR PEACE:

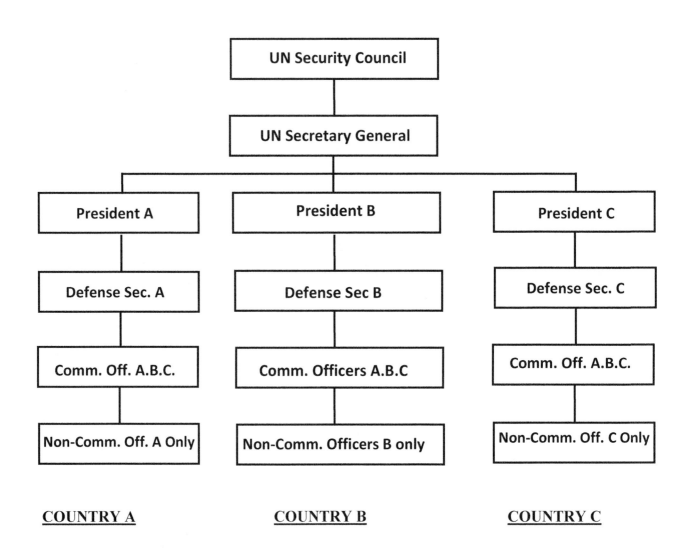

UN Security Council

UN Secretary General

President A	President B	President C
Defense Sec. A	Defense Sec B	Defense Sec. C
Comm. Off. A.B.C.	Comm. Officers A.B.C	Comm. Off. A.B.C.
Non-Comm. Off. A Only	Non-Comm. Officers B only	Non-Comm. Off. C Only

<u>COUNTRY A</u>   <u>COUNTRY B</u>   <u>COUNTRY C</u>

SEAL TWO

THE POLITICAL QUESTION AND GOD'S ANSWER

"Some day there will be a king who rules with integrity, and national leaders who govern with justice."

- (Isaiah 32:1)

Many governments today are in the process of trying to solve their various social, political and economic imbalances given a suitable political framework or system. The party systems of democracy have been relatively successful with some, but a majority of the evolving societies are still clamped down with ineptitude and setbacks despite. The various options or versions available are just not sustainable.

Like other systems tried, party democracies too have been truncated and abrogated by revolts on excuses of "bad government" at various times. Some bad government's malfeasances are: political exclusion, socio-economic marginalization, lack of sensitivity of government, arbitrariness of government, high cost of bureaucracy, bribery, corruption, graft, embezzlement, misappropriation, sit-tight leadership and powerful personalities over institutions, official high-handedness, nepotism, poor planning, unbalanced representation, misrule, mismanagement, in-transparency of governance, remoteness of government, discontinuity, etc., etc. These and more are just some of the so many issues and problems raised and attributable to inefficient systems of democracy in practice today.

As expressed above, many think "party" democratic systems of government still offer the best solutions to these problems. This somewhat is questionable, given our preamble. What then could suffice for sufficient answer, you ask? The answer, we believe, could be subsumed in this novel version of non-party democratic system of government we tag: *"Neutral-party System"*; otherwise *'N-party,'* for short. What could N-party be?

N-party could also pass as acronym for No, Nil, Non, or Neutral–party system of democracy. It is a brand of grassroots democracy in which representation is on zero, nil or no party basis (hence the name). How might N-party work, you ask? Observe the diagram below:

HEIRACHY IN THE N-PARTY SYSTEM:

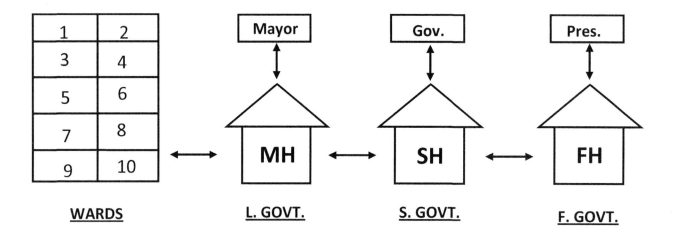

Take a hypothetical confederation. Let us assume it has a central government, and 10 equal (or homogeneous) provincial/regional governments, by population. Let each of the 10 provinces or regions also consist of 10 homogeneous local (or mayoral) governments by population too. And let each local (or mayoral) government consist of 10 homogeneous wards (or councils) by population still. This all for fairness, equity, and equal representation of candidates.

At the general elections, the wards or councils (as constituencies) would elect in - say, 10 candidates each - on zero-party basis, as representatives-elect into their respective mayoral houses of parliament at the local governments. These elections, as envisaged, could be marred save if carried out perhaps by a peculiar and novel electioneering system or process as explained now: This electoral process is to be aided by a novel and especial voting right and power we tag: the *"plurality of franchise"*. What could this all be?

It is an avowed international best practice that 'franchise' is that political right or power to elect and be elected, to vote and be voted for. This would be best upheld comparatively by this our new voting right and power: the *plurality of franchise*. Which defined is: *"that all qualified and registered voters may stand candidates simply by themselves and cast their votes freely, singularly and directly for themselves as a one-man individual contestant and be elected, as may for any other electorates (who also are empowered to stand freely and be voted) in any elections."* This in breakdown means **"parties"** [i.e., political candidates] can be as **"plural"** [numerous] as there are voters, and each voter **"reserves"** [can spend freely] his own vote. Hence we talk about a **"plurality of franchise"**. This is a fundamental rule of engagement in the entire N-party and its psephology. And this stands it out from all other political systems presently in practice. (It may be granted that civil society and pressure groups present candidates for election by consensus - as may any other - but patronage is self-willed and unenforceable by the law).

When general elections are conducted at the grassroots on *pluralism* basis as thus, say 10 highest poll winners are derived from each ward [or constituency] by simple majority to represent it in its mayoral house of parliament at the council. 100 such candidates would then converge into each of the mayoral houses across the federation (given 10 wards or councils make up each). General elections involving the public end here. Power of representation and elections is devolved to the representatives-elect onward in-house as a College.

On convergence in each of the mayoral houses, the new-elect representatives (MPs) would sit collectively to determine and fashion out their plans and programs for their term - say, a 5 or 6 years term. When their agendas have been collated and aggregated, the houses would each then sit to elect their Chief Executives (Mayors).

This may be done by an arrangement similar to the one explained earlier but different in certain respects. In all collegiate (or house) elections, candidates willingly may context and stand election within their houses, but would not however be allowed to cast their votes for themselves (as in the general elections). This avoids any foreseeable stalemates of self-voting. Also lot then would be drawn upon the polls as cast to determine the winners: allowing for the 'Hand of Providence' (or God) to determine ultimately the winners. This being so supported in the book of Proverbs 16:33 of Bible, which states: *"Men cast lots to learn God's will, but God himself determines the answer."* Asides, this too helps lend voice to, and takes care of, the rights and interests of minorities in the houses.

Granted elections being such as this, the mayoral houses next "elect" representatives frontwards into the provincial (or state) assemblies. If say 10 members are 'elected' frontwards by each mayoral house, we would then have 100 new MPs in each provincial house. The mayoral houses then would each have been reduced to 90 members.

Similarly, the provincial houses also determine their programs and plans and 'elect' their governors. Next, each then elects the 10 representatives frontwards into the national assembly. There would then be 100 new MPs in the federal house, and 90 remaining in each province.

The federal house also determines its own programs and agenda and 'elects' the president. With the federal, state, and mayoral offices completed, government business then begins.

The chief executives (President, Governors, and Mayors) can then appoint their cabinets, using technocrats or others, with all autonomy and non-interference from their houses. Bearing also in mind, that they would solely bear the brunt, and be held accountable and responsible for any flaws or mis-governance in the executives. And with respect to this may be deposed by the houses they involved from and to which they report and account to. This is the same that is empowered to oversee their governments and may raise 'votes of no confidence' against them in an eventuality. In some indictments bordering on corruption, theft, graft, or embezzlement of public funds, the direct culprits however would also be made to face the music in the courts of law.

However, as a balance, the heads of government would be allowed 3 month's grace to settle down in office before any impeachment proceedings may be made against them. And this can only be successful upon a 2/3rds majority vote against them in their houses.

As another defense, executive-heads are also allowed to retain an officer behind in their seats in the houses to represent and defend their cabinets before parliament and to participate in all parliamentary activities (including voting). These officers lose office to their principals when they are returned to parliament after an impeachment.

Pertinently too, any legislators (MPs) who leave parliament to take up appointments in the executives do so at the risk of their offices. Immediately they leave to take up appointments, elections are held in the overseeing subordinate houses they are elected to represent in the lower tiers to fill those vacancies. (The prerogatives of returning back to the houses belong only to executive-heads).

Germaine also is that in transitional elections (i.e., general elections at expiration of term) it is the parliaments that transit. The executives overlap (remain intact), until impeached in a vote of no confidence. Therefore, the government is a continuum. The seating chief-executives' seats in the constituents are therefore always uncontested and reserved in general elections.

After a chief-executive has been deposed, the parliament would convene to elect a new officer to continue the executive headship from amongst them by in-house voting. He too is also empowered with all grace and autonomy to retain or to fire any cabinet members for longevity of tenure or self-preservation in office. This continues until eventually a stable, flawless, and effective leadership is enthroned as foreseen in Isaiah 32:1 of Scriptures (quoted above). It must be mentioned here that it is the self-same resolves and agendas that are being pursued, only that the administrators are changing. Hence there are no fears of discontinuity or red tape once they got their acts right.

Notably, legislators in the houses - as of the executives - also would be subject to checks and balances as the arrows do indicate in our diagrams: Federal MPs would account and report back to their respective lower state houses; while provincial MPs would account and report back to the subordinate mayoral houses in the local government tiers. All these MPs may be impeached and deposed by 'votes of no confidences' brought upon them by these overseeing subordinate houses for any flaws, paving way for a replacement by elections. As of course, this has to be upon a 2/3rds majority vote against them in the house and after the usual 3 months' honeymoon grace to settle down in office.

Going by our trajectory, mayoral MPs at the least tiers might seem unilateral since having no overseeing subordinate houses to report or account back to structurally. This however might not be so. Legislators in these houses should by the enabling act be empowered in the constitution the ability to raise votes of no confidence among themselves for failings or flaws as to be spelt out. Upon an impeachable flaw raised against any member (MP) by other members in their house, the member is deposed by passing a majority 2/3rds against him/her in the house. This notably would be made possible only after the usual 3 months' grace.

When such errant MPs are rusticated, fresh members are immediately called up and sworn-in from the list of winners at the general elections at the beginning of term. This list should be held in care of house leaders of parliament. Thus thereby are freshmen convoked as new representatives-elect of their wards or constituencies from the grassroots into the mayoral houses.

Let us concisely look at all what we have said in a summary: Candidates freely stand elections in their constituencies directly for seats into the mayoral houses. In-house collegiate-type elections continue in the mayoral houses into the provincial houses; and then into the federal. All houses elect their chief executives from among the house members. And the chief executives appoint their cabinets freely and autonomously. All office holders are responsible and accountable back to the subordinate offices they evolved from and are elected to represent. The diagram above summarizes all this once again.

In concluding, our advocacy would not be complete without a closer look at some of the peculiar advantages of the N-party system of government over other systems of government – party or no party:

In the N-party, a simple plurality of votes only is needed to succeed in any elections, which makes it easier for someone to accede to leadership. Leveraging support to this also is that there would be minimal rigging since everyone is perceived in competition individually against others. You will agree it would be more difficult to rig an election when working alone and against all others in a rivalry than when in a bloc or party. In the event of any riggings or grafts however, the self-regulatory mechanisms of the N-Party do not allow any rooms for mediocrity rule over the better expertise or good sense of others – be it majority or minority. Retaining clout and office would simply be on merit and by individual best-efforts. N-party therefore places everyone on a level playing field.

The N-party system, in its principles of political pluralism and popular participation, more effectively allows for freedom of expression of opinions by empowering nonpartisanship, or enabling self-willed non-patronage of others, by guaranteeing liberties and rights and allowing for a down-to-earth grassroots representation of everybody - which no other systems probably guarantees in as much. (At best, the multi-party systems of government polarize opinions which may be roundly populist than down to earth or factual).

Expediency demands also that we mention here again that N-Party succession and replacement mechanisms do not lead to red tape. Contrarily, they lead to greater efficiency or better ways of doing things. We have argued in support of this and now reiterate that it is the same resolves or plans that are pursued, only that the administrators are changing for greater effectiveness. So, there could be no validation of red-tape or discontinuity.

N-Party on a closer scrutiny can be seen to have infused in it the best of modernistic systems of government as: republicanism, rationalism, libertarianism, objectivism, positivism, and egalitarianism, etc., etc. There are also traceable the elements of some of our past heritage African systems of government; such as, the Yoruba cabinet collectivism, compartmentalization, and *Providentialism*, etc. N-Party can thus be said to be a political hybrid with all the characteristics of diamond - God's quintessential answer for man's (and particularly Nigeria's) many woes in their good governance quests!

There obviously also are observable N-party's distinctive separation of powers, and checks and balances. The institutions are well entrenched and powerful over persons. And as never before known, roles are better separated one from another. The organs also are observably sovereign and supreme. There is ample opportunity for the various arms to operate and exercise authority within their judicial latitudes and yet under cooperative team spirit. Of particular note, the judiciary is unequivocally guaranteed independence and sovereignty – and so also presumably would be the press and the anti-graft agencies. This is an added plus for N-Party advocacy considering Nigeria's case.

A most veritable check and balance to be conjectured of and observed in the entire system and its environment is the subliming ideological and sociological philosophy of *"neutrality of representative"*. We should recall that elected officers were to be evolved on no party basis, and hence hypothetically, all candidates would act independently in line with their own dictates or along the lines of those of their sponsors. There thus would be ephemeral allegiances and alliances. This makes everyone bear no social contract towards anyone particularly, but towards everyone generally in the common good. This evokes both a sublime, charismatic leadership; and a neutral, critical follower-ship. This also creates both a check and balance that upstarts about a paradigm shift towards general excellence and perfectionism, with electorates competing against one another in perceived selflessness to earn clout. This awesome and compelling ideological, sociological, philosophical, and psychological checkmate and balance upon the populace is what we term: the ***"neutrality of representative."*** Interestingly, it also overwhelmingly makes government the art and essence of politics, rather than politics the art or essence of government, as hitherto. It also thereby lends it its full name: ***"Neutral-Party System";*** abbreviated, "N-Party".

Pen-ultimately, we would (re)-define democracy from our perspective as simply: *"a central consensus, flanked about by an array of divergent views or opinions."* Or, as someone put it still: *"a small hard core of common agreement, surrounded by a wide variety of individual differences. "*Indeed this definition is to be taken as a hard fact of life and of the real world. For in the real world, there are as many divergent views and opinions as there are peoples or populace. N-party apparently captures them all.

And finally, we ought now to have been able to conjecture or figure out how the N-party eases out the many woes and symptoms of "bad government" as listed out. We would realize it has zero tolerance for any forms of corruption or bad governance given its functionality and modus operandi. We therefore then submit that N-Party transcends all reasoning, time, creed, or culture. It best answers man's political quests from the ages and presumably throughout all ages to come.

ADDENDUM

The diagrams and discourse above may be augmented with an international tier assuming nations want to make representations into any international forums such as: the UN, EU, AU, ECOWAS, Commonwealth, etc. It could also be adjusted [reduced or increased] in order to suit each country's population size or resource capability. The principles are same as elucidated. And all the advantages of the N-party appertain.

SEAL THREE

THE CRIME AND INSECURITY PROBLEM AND GOD'S SOLUTION

"Teach a child how he should live, and he will remember it all his life".

- (Proverbs 22:6)

Daily we panic and worry over at the growing crime menace ravaging our societies with dismay. But should we really look on in despair, resigned to fate, at this social dilemma, and not try to proffer lasting solutions to it? The following are three of some of the causes and reasons of this quagmire:

One; there is the consideration of a child's upbringing. People with a negative or people with a positively-deficient upbringing tend to deviate to crime or criminal ways of eking out a livelihood.

Two; idleness, indolence, and joblessness also may lead some potentially agile and tactile people into crime for a livelihood. This is inclusive of individuals with a will to express their potentialities, but without an opportunity.

Three; there are the social miscreants or "no-goods". This group of persons is really the pain in the neck. They are the ones who cause the decay of social fabrics and lend cause to flagrant moral decadence no matter the pampering of the authorities. And they are the ones we really cannot but always have in our societies and in all generations.

Everywhere in the earth there are daily recorded robberies, armed banditry, attacks against places of worship, hooliganism, internet fraud, kidnapping, arson, pilferage, terrorism, rape, drug-handling, and what-have-you. All society is debased, and there seem no lasting solutions. The devil is set berserk in the hearts and minds of many it seems and love among men has waxed cold! But can there not really be a way out of this quagmire beyond gentle persuasions? What follows from us in this piece might suffice for a way out of the dilemma:

Youths or teens in our understanding are usually predominant, or predominate, in all these classes of deviants as outlined. They have to their vantage such potencies as zeal, vigor and strength - which some deploy wrongfully into crime because misguided or naïve. It might then be expedient and appropriate to (re)-orientate them on the right paths so that a culture of civility and near uprightness or crimelessness could evolve to the common good. How do we do this, you ask?

To do this effectively somewhat may require initiating a "corps" or some constabulary that would incorporate both police and other paramilitary drills in its curriculum. The end-purpose of this is to plough the zeal and prowess of the youths into some more useful and constructive purpose as curbing and monitoring or policing their neighborhoods for some token rewards.

This 'youth-corps,' - as the name implies - should recruit members while they are still young and impressionable - say from ages thirteen (13) to twenty-five (25). Recruitment should however be voluntary rather than enforced. Obviously, some parents - or even the potential recruits – may resent the idea for any reasons best known to them.

During school holidays or vacations or at weekends, the recruits could be rallied together in pockets of nearest places of best convenience for training, under a command structure [or body] set up for this, and tutored in the art of civics, the law, intelligence gathering, criminology, community policing, crime prevention and detection, martial arts, and any other such relevant drills. All relevant kits and other paraphernalia of office should be provided them by the corps at no costs to them. Importantly however, the corps is not to be uniformed!

After graduating from this preliminary training, the recruits should then have been well taught and learned enough to be useful citizens, assisting the police and other such security operatives in their lines of duty as 'freelancers' for a token wage. This ever leaves the corps-members free to engage in other pecuniary passions and interests of theirs unhindered. (This as said is a pastime and to be done at one's pace and in one's spare time upon graduation from training, the reason why it is "freelance").

From their least ranks the recruits would keep climbing up by promotions as they report information on crimes and criminals. With each reporting, the corps-member is promoted in rank and with income and may be decorated with medals or other honors as deserved - an inducement for them to continually redouble their efforts. (However, some may get nothing for none reporting and may remain un-promoted). This thus partly putting paid an end to the problem of unemployment and the virtue issue among youths in one fell swoop!

Note critically that the corps does not carry out wholesome police duties technically, nor are they some rival force to the police; they rather are a vigilante and watchdog over the citizenry and upon themselves. They provide information and lead to and through their corps' command on criminal activities, which will then redirect onward to the right authorities for their action. This then leaves them less vulnerable or at risk. They also do not bear arms unlike the regular police or paramilitary, but may carry communication sets. And with this in place, nations need not maintain such large bands of regular police or paramilitary forces.

In line to safeguard against any members being in league with criminals or in complicity of any sort by giving misleading, negotiated or prejudiced information on purpose or for any gains, or withholding part or whole information that they are privy to, or proven to be in possession of, such recruits would risk sanctions. Some of such sanctions may be: de-medaling, regimental demotions, wage deductions, suspensions, outright rustications; or what-have-you as punishments (depending on the gravity of the offence). This kind of esprit de corps or misdemeanor would not and should not be condoned! All offences and their penalties are better ranked and served round the recruits at training and periodically to keep them always in view.

For the well-serving graduates of the system - those who peak [pass out] upon attaining maturity age twenty-five (25); or top rank and have to be compulsorily retired before attaining maturity age - automatic conscription could be reserved them into any of the paramilitary forces of their choice. Other rewards and honors could be formulated and bestowed upon them by the State or corps command. Or they otherwise may continue with normal civilian life after service. They however are also reserved a willing reservoir or pool for any of the forces to be called upon in emergencies.

Conclusively, the crime and criminality problem should have known God's solution, or be reduced to the barest minimum, as successive generations of youths and teenagers mature into adulthood, giving rise to uprightness and near-crimelessness to the common good. This evidently because, as the Bible admonishes: *"teach a child how he should live, and he will remember it all his life"* (Proverbs 22:6).

This then is a permanent long-term palliative from God to the crime and insecurity problem plaguing our societies in addition to any other palliatives currently subsisting. And because we know that criminals are humans, living and having their being within society and not in some underground coven, they then can best be sought out and brought under the law by their most congenial peers or age grades – youths and teens, hence the call for this corps. It may take some while for this to yield full dividends as foreseeable, but the benefits and externalities will eventually rob off sooner than later.

SEAL FOUR

GOD'S NEW COMMON WEALTH

"God says, 'I will bring you lasting prosperity; the wealth of the nations will flow to you like a river that never goes dry ..."

- (Isaiah 66:12)

Consumables' prices raise worldwide each time demand for energy consumption is greater than the supply or production. And fall when energy is over-supplied or glutted. These imbalances in energy demand and supply nearly always cause trade-offs in price patterns of most goods and services rendered. That is, in some cases, goods and services that ordinarily would have generated wealth to some investors are thereby being relegated as "luxuries" in preference to other goods so-called "essentials".

Economies sustained by and reliant upon these purported 'luxury' goods and services in international trade thus recess. This recession helps only to create a super-imposition or lopsidedness of ideas on the kinds of goods and services to be produced locally. Unemployment and other social vices usually then follow as the factories producing 'luxury' goods close down and retrench staff. Money needed to meet the economic needs or demands of the common man thus becomes scarce and they cannot compete favorably in the market place with the wealthy few for goods and services being offered. Those citizens who can afford it seek escape abroad in an attempt to find greener pastures or relief. In so doing, they create a problem of brain-drain and intellectual paucity in the already pauperized home economies. This is the bane of slow development in emerging economies today. It is a vicious cycle of poverty, recession and depression.

In Nigeria (using Nigeria my country as case study), economic policies are as a result of movements in international oil and gas sales – our major source of income. The management of oil-related risks therefore is of prior importance to us. Oil and gas revenues (in our opinion) should therefore be managed in such ways that provide employment, growth and succor for our teeming unemployed in *"labor-intensive"* endeavors. The 3-tiers of government in gearing and sustaining the developmental effort should as facilitators open up the land and provide the enabling business environment by constructing more sea and air ports, extend road networks, railways, inland waterways, telephony and other communication networks, provide pipe-borne water, supply regular electricity, and maintain adequate security of lives and properties.

Public corporations and investments rightly are to be privatized by stock sales. Government's role should be only as facilitator - regulator or supervisor - and not as catalyst. Government's portfolio of investments – inclusive of ministries and departments, etc - and retinue of staff should be shrunken [reduced or down-sized] and re-engineered to generate own funding through commercialization of their services and operations, leaving government with lesser burden.

As some other governments have realized, our policy-makers too should realize that public-funded corporations and departments are usually paid their salaries and running expenses from public resources, no matter their performances; while their private-sector counterparts in a market economy must earn their value to retain hold on their clients. Any wonder they get creative through research and development!

Some economists have argued that inflation is caused by excess money supply. These scholars opine: money should then be regulated or pegged to grow with Gross Domestic Product (GDP). We argue to the contrary, that money peg is unadvisable; rather, the problem is with increasing volume of production or capacity. To keep our economy booming therefore, real production must be increased to equal up to quantum of fiduciary issue (money supply), vis-à-vis the rate of economic growth. So, to our learning and understanding, money de-pegging or deregulation with increased production will increase employment, encourage free trade, reduce inflation, and revive the economy; while money peg or regulation will do the converse.

It is also noted by some economists that a currency's velocity of exchange is the rate at which it circulates (or changes hands). We further add that asides this, velocity too determines or benchmarks capacity for growth [enlargement] of the economy. For instance, in Nigeria's case, a very rapid or fast velocity of naira exchange represents scarcity of money supply to meet growth. A rapid velocity thus thirsts for more money (i.e., monetary ease policies). Conversely, a slow velocity of naira exchange speaks of saturation of money supply. In an emerging economy like ours, the economy needs more volume [capacity] enlargement or more production and investments. While thirdly, an average velocity speaks of stability, or of even-paced development or full-capacity utilization.

In some other first pieces of advice to countries facing our kind of peculiar economic and financial challenges or seeking to grow wealth by increasing capacity, windfalls derivable from privatization or commercialization of public investments; or export receipts; or governments' deficit financing policies, etc., should be applied in monetizing entrepreneurs engaged in '*labor-intensive*' endeavors. In so doing government is grossly helping to empower economically the work force.

Furthermore, labor should be in *two (2) or three (3) shifts* to accommodate the teeming workforce; and liberalized by leaving freely to the vagaries of market forces. Free labor markets best allow market forces of demand and supply to equilibrate wages to be paid to employees by employers, and vice versa. Only incidences of frictional unemployment would be permissible as workers move from one job unto another.

A second open manner of empowerment for commercial endeavors would be through the open market (OMO): in which, money is released into the economy by the central bank buying bonds. In the event of such monetary empowerment of entrepreneurs, they would turn the cash over; thus revenues would be accruable - especially from *export receipts*. And thus shall these businesses be enriched and grow in scale. As commerce and industrialization boom locally, more workers would be needed, and more wages paid. The increased demand resultant from the expanded wages would further engender corresponding supplies and production from the other satellite firms to meet up. Gradually as this virtuous cycle continues, the economy would steadily pick up.

A third and most imaginative, effective, and open manner of managing and controlling money stock and the economy is again for national governments solely to run and operate *'financial Ponzi schemes'* as perpetuities for their citizens to subscribe to for investment capital to set up and run (their own) small and medium scale enterprises (SMEs). The 'Ponzi' works two-way as a monetary policy tool: On the one hand, it channels funds into the hands of ordinary citizens, which they may accumulate and direct into desired personal investments or SMEs. And on the other hand, it mops up excess liquidity in the economy back into the government's purse in the form of fees paid by all participants (or entrants). This, the government may then re-channel or redirect into the mainstream economy by any of the options or methods open to it (as in above). The continuing processes of releasing and mopping up money supply thus, would eternally avail funds or necessary capital to the real sectors for determinable and purposeful use.

We here support and call for the creation of more tax-havens. Possibly our whole nation should be a tax-haven! By this, minimal taxes and tariffs should be placed upon home goods to protect our infant industries so that their produces cost less relative to imports. Imports however (especially of goods with home substitutes) should particularly be sur-taxed over and above their home competitors so that they cost more and are discouraged. But these imports and their consumption should not be banned or outlawed, because competition enables product development and improvement. Necessarily, tariffs and taxes should preferably be applied at source and value-added so that they incidence on end-consumers. Income and whatever other taxes are however to be proportional, rather than regressive or progressive (which otherwise tends to be subjective and judgmental!)

Bank interest rates, ratios and requirements are to be left flexible and competitive so that they become lowered. Banks can thence facilitate commerce/investments, and create wealth with freer hand with capital or funds. With the liberty of banks and other financial houses to disburse loans will come a healthier and more robust financial sector to boost growth.

In furtherance of our free trade and free market advocacies, all subsidies, exchange controls, cartels, or any other inflexibilities, etc, are to be done away with. There must necessarily be total and complete liberalization, deregulation and non-censorship in manufacturing and production, as in trade. Trade by specialization and exchange should therefore be the order of the day. What can best be produced locally thus be produced and exchanged for other goods and services better produced in other lands. All such inter-trading countries would ultimately save on costs, save wastages, and save energies and skills. Nations will then be enjoying the wealth of the earth as best they can afford.

Stock markets as we know intermediate investment capital. Capital made ready by whatever monetization of the citizens and channeled into the economy in investments on the stock market creates a stock market boom, given that such capital expands business and industrial activity. And as commerce and commercial activities blossom and become enlarged, so will prices of goods and services decline in breakneck competitiveness or price wars. Thus inflation reduces. Imports would reduce if discouraged by taxing higher over locally produced goods; but exports would generate additional incomes for firms if taxed lesser - creating favorable terms of trade and favorable balance of payments. The monies thereby made available to those business concerns would bring down bank lending rates as fewer loans are demanded. The lowered costs of capital would also induce more investments and engender more employment. With increased employment, more wages would be paid and consumption increased. The increased demand would in turn booster more production and further investments. The spiraling situation would so greatly create jobs everywhere and for everyone! Indeed, we shall experience also an influx of brains and skills from abroad into our markets seeking for opportunities, known as *"foreign direct investments"*.

Evidently, so much investment capital would be made available such that reserves pile up and the naira gains value and strength and is at par with world top currencies. This probably is how nations of the world can attain the much desirable but elusive ***purchasing power parity (PPP)*** in international finance.

While yet achieving currency rate parity, we shall also inadvertently have divested our economy from a sole-export earner to a multi-faceted one. And evidently we too shall be setting up investments abroad like other advanced industrial societies. What is needed done is to: ***make our nation and the whole earth one phenomenal free-trade-territory for international***

exchanges! Then would our economies not have to cringe any more under the pangs of price and revenue fluctuations in any one product – oil and gas, as in the case of Nigeria. Other exports would buffer up the economy!

All things being equal, all nations following in the steps of this discourse would forever bask in this common wealth as already promised of God in the Holy Scriptures wherein He declares: *"I will bring you lasting prosperity; the wealth of the nations will flow to you like a river that never goes dry"*. Almighty God Himself invariably saying that the economies of nations would never have to recess and ever be in wealth!

Albeit, one snag to achieving all this loftiness might be that not everyone is "economic-minded." There are a couple few whom when monetized would spend on *'consumables'* rather than *'investments.'* It therefore behooves on governments to bring the government closer to their peoples by carrying them along on these programs so they may run with them on hitting ground.

SEAL FIVE

GEARING AND SUSTAINING DEVELOPMENT GOD'S WAY

"The basic needs of life are these: water, fire, iron and salt, flour, honey, and milk, wine, clothing and oil. All these are good for those who are devout, but they turn into evils for sinners"

- (Sirach 39:26-27)

Development and growth in most economies is known to be as a result of skilled citizenry coupling with available natural material resources to produce outputs that meet needs [demands]. Firstly, it is thought development should not only meet needs, it should also supersede any environmental expenses arising there-from. In other word it must be economical.

Secondly, it is also thought by scholars that development should enhance the beauty of the environment in which it is taking place to be sustainable. It must add aesthetic value.

Thirdly and lastly, development while meeting present generations' growth must not jeopardize future generations' own growth needs. It must be forward looking.

To ginger and sustain the process of growth and development, we advice nations should first debate and rank their needs for growth in every generation; they then may pursue these strategically. Some of the objectives or goals for prior consideration are as has been pinpointed generally in this book. Some others more are as follows:

Foremost and primarily, for development to be sustained smaller families are to be canvassed by governments and population management are to be encouraged. Smaller families enable wealth go round more evenly plus its attendant checks on over-population. When God said to man in the beginning of creation: be fruitful, multiply, replenish, subdue, and have dominion over the earth and creation, He meant: man should take charge and manage the earth such as to preserve, protect, sustain, and maintain its biodiversity and ecology.

If you take for instance in the delta regions of south-south Nigeria (or others), restiveness and militancy in these oil-producing communities are caused by oil spillages and cannot be resolved wholesomely until and unless such projects are jettisoned for present and future generations' own needs to be met. These people depend on the land and agriculture for an existence, and this must not be jeopardized for present gains. In the place of oil exploitation, liquefied natural gas (LNG) should instead be prospected and piped to homes and offices. LNG is less catastrophic to prospect and equally as serving if properly engineered and researched. Remember again, development must be economical, enhance the beauty of the environment, as well as be forward-looking to be sustainable.

It behooves therefore also upon all governments and peoples to detest and curb environmental degradation in the earth through the exploitation of non-renewable mineral energy resources (i.e., coal, oil, and nuclear, etc.). Alternatively, bio-mass, solar, rain, wind, sea, etc., should be explored. Proactively avoiding global warming, ozone layer depletion and exposure of the environment to pollution should be prioritized by all nations and people. This otherwise cause the degradation of the environment, creates in-excludable costs for all, and is anti-development, going by our definitions.

As greenhouse gases, chlorofluorocarbon (CFC), and all such other industrial pollutants, are released into the air, the ozone layer depletes and the sun's effects intensify upon the earth; causing snow to melt and more volumes of water released into the seas and oceans. This results in greater volumes of rainfall and higher sea levels, causing flooding (which effects we see all over the world today). For us in the rainforest belts of Africa, we should consider exporting the excess waters to the deserts up north! - talking about the Sahel and the Sahara. This could be achieved, for instance in Nigeria, just as oil is transported in pipes from the south of our country to the north to be refined. This way we would be putting a check to desert encroachment and perennial droughts in the north and checkmating flooding in the south.

To support preservation again, we argue that the earth is our home and belongs to all humanity together. It is therefore a public good like the air we breathe in and out. Earth preservation and conservation then is everyone's right and responsibility to defend and to protect. The earth as our right duly implies certain responsibilities, obligations and duties upon us. Because, firstly and as validly or rightly given in both instances, there is no right without responsibility and no responsibility without obligation or duty. And secondly, the rights of one are limited by the rights of every other; we therefore conclude that those who destroy, deface, or tamper with the earth in whatever form impinge and infringe upon the collective rights of the whole humanity, and must rightly be checked! We suggest this by monetary means', as: tolls, levies and fines, etc.

Land tenure systems also are to be reformed by in-securing land to mortgagers, as hitherto. Our governments rather should solely be granting rental mortgages to all estate users for specific periods only. After which tenure, title reverts back to government to be re-bargained or repurchased as the case may be. Our argument in support of this again is that: land, like the Earth, is a public good. The implication of this is that, this resource should be centrally owned and sold for fairness and equity sake. Hence this calls for government overly proprietary right to estates.

Also in another piece of advice to the emerging economies of Africa and Asia whose land

and environmental resources are still virgin, we propose that they pursue programs that engender "service-oriented" industrialization – like ***modernized agriculture and agro-businesses*** - to protect their atmospheres and those of the world from further pollution from heavy manufacturing processes. Especially for countries in the tropics, solar and hydro energy may be further researched and developed for export to grow and invigorate their economies.

Furthermore to this, the Good News Bible or the Living Bible (and such other versions), provide wisdom, knowledge and insight for revitalization and ingenuity to be further researched by man. For instance, in Genesis 30:37–43, Jacob founded the practice and application of genetic engineering to farming. The Book of Tobit 11:8 provides advice on how to restore blindness or impaired sight. Malachi 3:10 provides insight into wealth and riches creation. Gospel music has proven spiritual cure in the Bible for mental illnesses like King Saul's (1Samuel 16:23). And James 5:14-16 & Revelation 22:2, among others, give counsel and guidance on healing for sick or ill persons. Many other such problems are already provided solutions to by God in the Holy Bible to be further researched and developed!

To recap all this in one word, governments are advised to sacrifice development for environmental quality and protection; salvage the environment from all kinds of desolation and pollution such as: oil spillages, global warming, desertification, ozone layer depletion, etc., which could impose costs on all. And finally, authorities are to seek and research alternatives to replicate exploitation of mineral fuel and other non-renewable resources.

SEAL SIX

LEGAL REFORMS BY GOD

"The Sovereign LORD has filled me with his spirit. He has chosen me and sent me to bring good news to the poor, to heal the broken hearted, to announce release to captives and freedom to those in prison".

- (Isaiah 61:1)

- There is to be no clandestine activities or occultism permitted in the earth under any guise.

- Legal age of responsibility, accountability and adulthood should be nineteen (19) years of age.

- Marriage is meant for adult persons only. Therefore minors (those under 19 years of age) may not marry; only adults may marry.

- Minors should not smoke, nor drink alcohol, nor have sex legally. To do either of these before attaining to adult age would be a penal offence under the law.

- Owners are to be responsible for their pets willingly.

- Parents are to be responsible for the offences of their minor children irrespective.

- If minors engage in contractual agreements or engagements (like employment, etc), their parents would be held accountable and responsible if they fail in their obligations or default on the contract.

- By the law, orphanages may not and should not mature their wards off until maturity age nineteen (19).

- One should not take life, except it be an "unwanted pregnancy". We argue that a fetus is an integral part of the carrier and can be likened to cancer or fibroid growing in the stomach. Its stay in the womb is at the discretion of the carrier, and so it may be removed as any other disease or growth no matter how come about. But a newborn's life is established - it is independent; and so has the full rights of a living soul! It must therefore not be tampered with under any guise or circumstances.

- It should however be noted that though abortion may be a sin, it is not an offence or crime. Man's concern should be to punish crimes and offences and leave any sins unto God's judgment.

- A crime may be defined as a wrong unto a third-party (man or state), while a sin is a wrong unto God. Abortion is a wrong unto God and oneself, not third-party.

- To make up for sins unto God, one may plead mercy or make restitution in prayers. But to compensate or make right a crime unto men or the state, payment be made in cash or in kind (as will be elaborated upon later).

- If two adult persons of opposite sex willingly have a child outside wedlock, they would both equally be responsible for the upkeep of the child up until nineteen (19) years of age. From infancy, the child could stay with the mother up until twelve (12) years of age. From there on, it could stay with the father till age nineteen (19).

- If a minor (or two minors) have a child, the responsibility of the child rests upon the parents of the minors irrespective. However, the minors take full charge upon their attainment of maturity age nineteen (19).

- If a minor or other is raped, the rapist shall bear the entire health [trauma and abortion] expenses of the raped as punishment.

- If any woman is raped, the entire upkeep expense of the child resultant rests with the father. However, the mother nurses the child from birth until age two (2) years old. Custody may then revert to the father there-on.

- If any woman is gang-raped, the entire upkeep expense of the child resultant rests with the gang evenly. However, such offspring belongs to, and bears the name of the biological father (upon medical certification). The father is to have custody of the child to care for from age two (2) as in above, with upkeep contributions from the gang evenly.

- Cloning, especially researches to clone humans and other living beings, is to be done away with forever. It is evil and satanic, and an aberration and a perversion before God - a sin-act punishable by damnation to hell!

- Similarly, bestiality, cunnilingus, anal sex, and all such sexual perversions must be commonly denounced and renounced. They are a debasement of both animal and human dignity; and are sin-acts of sodomy unto God and man! What God grants is liberty, not unbridled freedom!

- So are same–sex marriages and sex-transplants to be condemned. The accomplices in these sins are equally also as guilty as the doers in judgment before God. They are all Sodomites and perverts before God, and are all damnable to hell! Their acts and practices should best be proscribed, forbidden, abrogated, and outlawed forever! They are as magic or black arts – corrupt and sinful! And are to be done away with.

- (Granted these very stern, forthright and passionate warnings, some thick-skinned, stiff-necked and die-hard 'Judases' would still do to the contrary. Speculatively, they would still choose to make clones for sex, industrial, domestic, or for whatever purposes best known to them! And some day, the clones would rise against them and cause a colossal war that would destroy the earth and all earthling beings! Therefore, beware! Be alert!! Be on your guard!!! Heaven and earth will pass away, but these words will remain!)

- Nevertheless, for developmental purposes, cloning science and technology however may be applied in researches to regenerate dead (or dysfunctional) cells in the cure of cancer, gangrene, spinal or brain diseases, etc. – what is objectionable is that it must not be used to replicate whole beings for substitution purposes, nor to improvise God or God's beings! (Remember the admonitions of Proverbs 29:1, which says: *"if you get more stubborn every time you are corrected, one day you will be crushed and never recover"*).

- It would be an offence to wield a weapon at anyone for whatever reasons. That is to say, no one may bear arms except the police and army. Anyone wanting to defend themselves is better advised to learn unarmed self-defense or martial arts. The only exceptions to this rule again are: *law agents,* ***"enforcing"*** *the law,* ***"under duty"***, *and under the* ***"codes of conduct"*** *of their duties.* In contravention to this, these also would be subject to the law and can be sued [prosecuted] accordingly.

- Private security outfits (security corporations), which may or may not employ ex-servicemen in their services, may also bear arms provided they are trained in their use. They too would then be subject to the laws regarding arms use and misuse or abuse.

- The police are to be decentralized. Each mayoralty is fully to run its own command to police it. Such are in the best positions to understand their own terrains, and are most suitable to understand and police their own people.

- Incarcerations or imprisonments or quarantines, as punishment for offences, are to be abolished (excepting for quarantines on medical or mental grounds). Alternatively to this, **all offences are to be monetized** [that is, paid for in terms of money or in kind as alluded to above]. Thereby shall the nations be making savings of public monies on maintaining criminals in prisons.

- Monetized charges are preferably to be charged as 'percentage-worth of estate' upon culprits, rather than as absolutes; but that is not to rule out absolutes altogether (as might need be).

- Also, compensations or restitutions for miscarriages of justice or misjudgment should be monetized to the wrongfully convicted.

- Corporal punishments, the death penalty, and such harsh judgments in the Nigerian (or others') laws should therefore be abrogated and done away with. Reason is that, if you abuse or take life wrongfully by misjudgment, there's no way you could compensate the adjudged sufficiently thereafter. Therefore capital or corporal offences in our laws (common or martial) should carry monetized charges as suggested.

- Inability to pay for offenses shall lead to declaration of bankruptcy on the convict. Two types of bankruptcy can be declared: (1) Business bankruptcy and (2) Legal bankruptcy. Legal bankruptcy is insolvency arising from a court judgment [criminal litigation action]. Both types of bankruptcy would limit the convict as given in law.

- All bankrupts (whether business or legal) would have to serve their charges in capacities or duties the state provides until their charges are liquidated (or discharged). That is, the bankruptcy will not be discharged until upon full payment of bills owed.

- Convicted persons could be swapped, exchanged, or replaced with or by another. They may also be "bought off" by payment of the bills on their charges by anyone (or self) at any time. Otherwise such persons would have to serve until "discharged".

- Convicts even while serving sentence, are free citizens and may not be discriminated against by employers. They may seek employment anywhere to earn decent wages. However, their employers must remit their "dues" from source to the courts or state until discharged. (This calls for collaboration between employers, the state, and the convict).

- Under no circumstance may a convict "jump bail". To jump bail would attract an imprisonment term. This is the only time the incarceration or imprisonment penalty may be justifiable. If the convict however later shows remorse or is penitent, their sentences may be commuted to cash or kind [monetized], or pardoned on the prerogative of mercy.

- All lands are to belong to the central congressional authority. Provincial and mayoral governments are to be delineated territories or bounds by the central authority.

- Citizens of any mayoralty may buy and develop land irrespective from the mayoralty authorities for a lease term of hundred (100) years.

- The governmental authorities should retain proprietary rights and could reclaim their land rights at any time, but must have to pay commensurate and adequate compensation to the deed owners if reclaimed before the hundred (100) years agreed.

- Land-owners however may develop or resell their estates before the time redeemable by the authorities.

- Mineral resource(s) found on any premises prompting redemption by government must be adequately compensated for by the governmental authorities to the leaseholders – perhaps as percentage royalties, until term expires. Or the lessees may exploit such resources as their rightful enterprises, to pay taxes on returns to the mayoral authorities.

- Mayoralties are to be empowered right to collect taxes, tolls, fines, rates, and revenues, etc., (since these are at the grassroots) and then pass up to the other tiers.

- Every generation of peoples upon earth is to have laws and agreements binding them for a set time. Agreements or bonds reached by that generation of people should bind for that time of people only. That is, no generations are allowed to jeopardize future generations' own rights with its sealed bonds or templates with themselves (or with other nations) any longer than for their epoch. A political epoch or generation by definition is anything between 5 years (minimum) to 6 years (maximum) by God!

- After a 'generation' has elapsed as set, the incumbent House (of Assembly) of the new era is to sit and reach agreements on general templates, policies and plans they shall be run by until the next epoch; and on and on.

- Any 'generations of people' therefore could revisit and review the templates and agreements made upon it by its progenitors - whether they are unilateral, bilateral or multilateral - inclusive of, but not limited to: interstate relations or pacts, social, political, economic and developmental templates and plans, etc.

- All nations under the international community necessarily should append to and abide by all these. (In contravention to implementing these lofty ideals, nations and peoples everywhere might as well be chasing the wind looking for solutions to problems that have already been given answers to by God.

SEAL SEVEN

CHURCH REFORMS BY GOD

Then the seventh angel blew his trumpet, and there were loud voices in heaven saying, 'The power to rule over the world belongs now to our God and his Messiah, and he will rule forever and ever!' - (Revelation 11:15)

- There is only one God and He is "the TRINITY!" That is: God the Father, Holy Spirit, and Son - as One! It is wrong for anybody to worship any other, or none!

- There is therefore no such thing with God as: 'freedom of religion.' All should and must worship Almighty God! This may not sound politically correct, but it is the only spiritually correct given truth! Remember, God is not a democrat, but a Theocrat. And as such He rules by ordinances and commandments which are eternally true and cannot be challenged. If He says He alone must be worshipped, He alone then must be worshipped! (Exodus 20:3).

- To challenge God's statutes or commandments is to sideline Him for the self, or to have other altars other than Himself – whether Shinto, Buddha, Allah, or Krishna, etc.! This is characteristic of the "children of disobedience" spoken of variously in the Bible, and a symptom of backsliding from true worship of the One God! (Exodus 20:4-6).

- Any building or medium of broadcast for Church worship is built and sustained by the collective purse (whether known or unknown) to the pastorate and therefore is the "House" of God! Nobody therefore has absolute right, authority or power in the 'House' of God, but God only! Church ministries therefore must be in-subordinated under God through Christ, and Christ under God.

- Since nobody has absolute right or power in the House of God, but God only, nobody has any right or absolute authority therefore to bar, deter or censor anyone from 'worshipping' there-from, but God. If anyone deters someone, he is scattering and not gathering, for: "*whoever is not against for us is for us*" (Mark 9:40). The house of God is meant for all comers – saints and sinners alike; and should be a reformation ground for change unto holiness and godliness. Therefore nobody should be barred, deterred, or censored from worshipping there-from, **provided they keep with the tenets of the Faith as laid down by the Bible.**

- Church leadership succession processes may be patterned after the *'Neutral-Party system'* elucidated upon earlier in seal two of this book. This may be adapted to suit each Church's principle or creed of faith (in-so-far as God is given liberty to ultimately determine the outcome of their choices by lot cast).

- Church leaderships therefore should constantly be under scrutiny by the laity to make sure they abide by and keep with the tenets of the Faith according to the Bible. If not, they may be defrocked and replaced by the ballot.

- Note rightly that God does not harbor malice, nor is angry with anyone indefinitely. Therefore if erring leaders or workers show remorse, they may be revalidated to contest and may again hold office. Having this in mind that the Holy Bible says:

"People learn from one another, just as iron sharpens iron." (Proverbs 27:17).

- Church money is God's money and should be used for God's work. It is one of the corporate social responsibilities of the church and part of God's work to cater for widows, orphans and elderly persons. All churches need to be alive to this responsibility as some Churches already are. We give kudus to those Churches!

- It is wrong for any ministers to deep hands into God's purse unauthorized. If at all, all ministers - from the founder(s) or superintendent(s) to the least workers - should be salaried! This will encourage workmanship, and perhaps this would also help check the fraud and avarice sometimes observable in the House of God or Church.

- Churches, as religious bodies, are charity and non-profit organizations and are therefore to remain tax-exempt. But if they run investments, then their investments may be taxed by the state.

- The order of the Trinity is not God the Father, Son, and Holy Spirit as erroneously believed. But rather: God the Father, Holy Spirit, and Son, in that order! Authors and users of the Bible alike should please take note and make amends

- Water baptism is by immersion in water, signifying death to sin and resurrection to newness of birth from sins. It can be observed privately at home in a water-tub or bath; and not necessarily in some pool – nor by some clergy.

- God instituted marriage by joining the first humans in the Garden of Eden (Genesis 2:24). Therefore all persons are expected to marry, without exception.

- Chastity and celibacy oaths though are good, but no oaths of celibacy or chastity made known to anyone other than God are acceptable by God! All Church ministries are therefore advised to keep their celibacy and chastity oaths private by not institutionalizing or advertising them in creeds. It however may be preached on the pulpit.

- All Church ministries must make allowances for their congregations to make confessions to third parties of their sins – making for peace of mind and healthy living of such persons.

EPILOGUE

The people who walked in darkness have seen a great light. They lived in a land of shadows, but now light is shining upon them.

You have given them great joy, LORD; you have made them happy. They rejoice in what you have done, as people rejoice when they harvest their corn or when they divide captured wealth.

For you have broken the yoke that burdened them and the rod that beat their shoulders. You have defeated the nation that oppressed and exploited your people, just as you defeated the army of Median long ago.

The boots of the invading army and all their bloodstained clothing will be destroyed by fire.

A child is born to us! A son is given to us! And he will be our ruler. He will be called "Wonderful Counselor," "Mighty God," "Eternal Father," "Prince of Peace."

His royal power will continue to grow; his kingdom will always be at peace. He will rule as King David's successor, basing his power on right and justice, from now until the end of time. The LORD Almighty is determined to do all this. (ISAIAH 9:2 – 7).

Printed in Great Britain
by Amazon